BARBARA McCLINTOCK

ALONE IN HER FIELD

BARBARA McCLINTOCK

ALONE IN HER FIELD

BY DEBORAH HEILIGMAN

ILLUSTRATED BY JANET HAMLIN

Scientific American

BOOKS FOR YOUNG READERS

W. H. FREEMAN AND COMPANY ◆ NEW YORK

Book design by Debora Smith

Scientific American Books for Young Readers is an imprint of
W.H. Freeman and Company, 41 Madison Avenue
New York, New York 10010

Library of Congress Cataloging-in-Publication Data

Heiligman, Deborah.

Barbara McClintock: Alone in Her Field / by Deborah Heiligman;

illustrated by Janet Hamlin.

ISBN 0-7167-6536-5 (hard).—ISBN 0-7167-6548-9 (soft)

[1. McClintock, Barbara, 1902-1992. 2. Geneticists. 3. Women—Biography.] I. Title.

QH429.2.M38H45 1994

575.1'092—dc20

[B]   94-6542

                                                                                                          CIP

                                                                                                          AC

Printed in the United States of America
10 9 8 7 6 5 4 3 2 1

For Jonathan
—he knows why. D.H.

THANKS TO: Lydia Brontë for permitting me to use her taped interview with Barbara McClintock; Clare Bunce, Susan Cooper, and Dr. Robert Martienssen of Cold Spring Harbor for digging, remembering, and explaining; Marjorie Bhavnani for sharing memories of her aunt; Evelyn Fox Keller, John Tyler Bonner, Pat Manning and Jonathan Weiner for reading and checking the manuscript for accuracy; Aaron Weiner for being my first (terrific) reader; Benjamin Weiner for sharing me with Barbara McClintock; and Nancy Laties Feresten for lovingly shepherding the book through every stage.

CONTENTS

INTRODUCTION

How would you feel if you made a great scientific discovery and nobody believed you? What if you tried to explain your discovery, and other scientists looked at you as if you were crazy? What if they still didn't believe you a year later? Five years later? Twenty years later?

That's just what happened to one of the greatest scientists of our time. Her name was Barbara McClintock.

Some people might have yelled and screamed until others understood. Other people would have been so discouraged and embarrassed, they would have given up. They might have decided they were wrong, and looked for a new problem in science to study. Or they might have quit science altogether.

Barbara McClintock did not yell or scream. She did not give up, either. She just kept on working. She knew she was right, and she knew that eventually others would see it too. "I knew it would all come out in the wash," she once said.

Barbara McClintock worked, alone, twelve hours a day, six days a week, month after month, year after year. She worked for thirty years before the world recognized the amazing discovery she had made.

What kind of person is happy to work alone, even though no one understands what she is doing? The kind of person Barbara McClintock was from the time she was a baby.

CHAPTER 1

The Wrong Name

From the time she was a baby, Barbara McClintock did not fit the mold. She broke it.

In the beginning, she wasn't even called Barbara. *Eleanor* McClintock was born on June 16, 1902, in Hartford, Connecticut. Her father, Thomas McClintock, was a doctor. Her mother, Sara McClintock, was a professional pianist, a writer, and a painter. Sara and Tom already had two children, Marjorie, four, and Mignon, two.

Baby Eleanor was different from the other two McClintock girls. She was also different from any baby Sara and Thomas had ever known. She rarely cried. She didn't ask for attention. She didn't like to be held or cuddled, the way most babies do. She liked being alone. Sara would put Eleanor on a pillow on the floor, give her one toy, and leave. Baby Eleanor stayed on the floor by herself, perfectly happy.

After living with their new baby for a few months, Thomas and Sara decided they had made a mistake. They had given her the wrong name! "My mother and father realized I wasn't going to be their idea of an Eleanor," Barbara McClintock explained years later. "They thought I was going to be something else. To them 'Eleanor' seemed like a delicate name. They knew I wasn't going to be sweet and gentle.

I was going to be much stronger. 'Barbara' sounded like a stronger name." So when she was four months old, Sara and Thomas McClintock changed their baby's name from Eleanor to Barbara. They thought that name was a better fit for the person they were getting to know.

Sara just could not feel close to this independent, uncuddly little girl. She did not become attached to her the way mothers usually become attached to their babies.

The problem with Barbara upset Sara, who was already having a difficult time. Sara had grown up in a wealthy family, and she was not prepared for all the work it took to run a house and raise children.

Thomas McClintock was just starting his medical practice. He worked long, hard hours for very little pay. As a new doctor, he had to build up his reputation, so he took on patients who couldn't pay, or who couldn't pay on time. Equipment was expensive, so much of the money he did earn had to go for medical and surgical tools. Turn-of-the-century doctors made house calls, which took up more time than seeing patients in an office. So, in addition to the big job of taking care of the children and the house, Sara also gave piano lessons to help make ends meet. Thomas took care of the babies in the little time he had left over so Sara could play music, write poetry, and paint.

Then, when Barbara was a year and a half old, Sara gave birth to another child, a boy this time, called Tom.

Having four young children was more than Sara and Thomas could manage. Something had to be done.

Sara was very close to Marjorie and Mignon, but her relationship with Barbara had not gotten any better now that Barbara was a toddler. Having one less child would make Sara's life easier—especially if that child was an added strain.

So Sara and Thomas decided to send Barbara away for a while. When she was two and a half, Barbara went to live with Thomas's sister Carrie and her husband, William, who was a wholesale fish merchant in Massachusetts. She ended up living there off and on until it was time for her to go to elementary school.

Although it may sound awful to be sent away from your family, Barbara had wonderful times with her aunt Carrie and uncle William. Perhaps she was even happier there than at home. While Sara McClintock was strong and high-spirited, Carrie King was sweet and gentle. Barbara loved her aunt Carrie and uncle William very much, and they adored her. In fact, they wanted to adopt her. Her mother might have agreed, but, as Barbara said later, "My father wouldn't have it."

One of the things Barbara loved most about living with the Kings was going out with her uncle to sell fish. Once a week, early in the morning, Barbara climbed into the horse-drawn carriage next to Uncle William. They would drive to the fish market, buy fish, load them into the carriage, and ride into the country. In those days, before big stores and supermarkets, many people bought food and goods from peddlers who sold their wares door-to-door.

Uncle William was a great big man with a great big voice. As he came to a house on his route, he would boom, "Do you want any

fish?" Barbara would watch eagerly to see if the woman of the house would come running out to buy some fish.

Within a couple of years, Uncle William bought a motor truck to replace his horse and carriage. Henry Ford had started building cars in the United States only a few years earlier, in 1903, so getting a new truck was an exciting event for everyone, including Barbara.

Uncle William's truck broke down a lot, but that was part of the fun. Barbara loved to watch her uncle fiddle with and fix the motor. From that time on she loved to figure out how things worked.

Barbara went back home to Connecticut sometimes for visits. Coming home was difficult for Barbara. Time apart didn't help Barbara and her mother understand each other any better. Sara still couldn't accept that it was not Barbara's nature to be sweet and gentle like her sisters. Barbara felt her mother's disapproval and resented her for it. One time, when Barbara was about three, Sara wanted to hug her. Barbara ran away, screaming. She hid behind the living-room curtains, which hung from the ceiling to the floor. "No, no!" she cried. "Don't touch me!" From that day on, Barbara refused to let her mother touch her.

Barbara did enjoy being with her father very much. They both loved machines and tools, and they loved fixing things together. Barbara thought of this as work—and she took it very seriously. Thomas loved to tell this story about Barbara: It seems that when she was five, Barbara asked her father for her own set of tools. He happily bought her some tools—toy tools. Barbara was very disappointed. She wanted real tools just like her father had.

"Tom and I were my father's children; Marjorie and Mignon were my mother's children," Barbara once explained.

Although Barbara might have been happier with her aunt Carrie as a mother, in some ways she was lucky that Sara was her mother. Sara had a mind of her own, and was very different from the other mothers of that era. As Barbara grew up, it was clear that she was very different from most turn-of-the-century girls.

CHAPTER 2

❦

"I Was an Oddball"

By the time Barbara was six years old and ready to go to school, Thomas McClintock was bringing in a good salary as a doctor. Barbara moved back with her family, and they all moved to Brooklyn, New York. Today, Brooklyn is a crowded city. But back in the early 1900s, there were wide open spaces; it was like the country. Behind the McClintocks' house were fields where Barbara and her sisters and brother often played. It was very difficult for Barbara to adjust to being back with her family. She missed her aunt and uncle very much. But one thing that brought her happiness was running through the fields, catching butterflies. That's where she fell in love with nature. She loved the freedom of being outside, of running and jumping and playing. But most of all she was fascinated by butterflies, and other insects, and plants.

The McClintock children had a lot of freedom, but Sara also taught them responsibility. Posted in the bathroom was a list of weekly chores. Each of the children had to help out cooking, cleaning, and doing other jobs around the house.

Although Sara and Thomas McClintock expected their children to follow their rules, they themselves did not always follow the rules other people made. They were very different from other parents of

that time (and this time too!). For one thing, they thought that going to school was only a part—and sometimes a small part—of growing up.

As soon as they moved to Brooklyn, Thomas called the school officials. He told them that his children were not to be given homework. Six hours in school should be enough time to teach his children what they needed to know. He wanted Marjorie, Mignon, Barbara, and Tom to be free to do whatever they wanted after school. He didn't want them stuck inside doing homework.

Not only that, but if the McClintock children had a good reason, they could stay home from school. One year, Barbara discovered she loved to ice-skate. So her parents bought her the best skates and the best skating outfit they could afford. If it was a good ice-skating day, Barbara stayed home from school to skate on the pond in nearby Prospect Park.

Another year Barbara came home from school crying every day. When her parents asked her why, she said it was because her teacher was ugly, "inside and out." So they took her out of school for the rest of that year!

Above all else, Sara and Thomas McClintock felt that their children should be who they were, not who other people thought they should be. They respected their children and their differences. However, Sara did worry about Barbara. She was so very different from other girls her age.

Rather than play with her sisters and other girls, Barbara liked to spend a lot of time alone. She loved to be by herself and just think about things. From the time she was very small, Barbara was trying to figure things out. One day Sara was crushing strawberries for strawberry shortcake. "Now I know where blood comes from," said Barbara. "It comes from strawberries!"

When she wasn't thinking about things, or reading, Barbara loved to play sports with her brother and his friends. In those days boys did boy things and girls did girl things. Barbara thought those categories were stupid. She wanted to play with the boys in her neighborhood. So she did. She climbed trees and played baseball, football, and volleyball.

Years later she said, "What you have to understand about people is that they don't always make sense. They don't always fit the mold." When you don't fit the mold, you often have to break the rules. Girls' clothes were terribly inconvenient for Barbara. Under their dresses girls wore bloomers, a kind of baggy long underwear made of delicate, frilly material. Barbara told her mother these clothes wouldn't do—they were too easily ruined. She insisted that she needed better clothes for playing. Sara didn't understand, but she gave in—as she usually did when her children insisted on something. When the dressmaker came to the house to make dresses for the girls, she made bloomers for Barbara out of the same sturdy material as her dress.

Other people were sometimes shocked by Barbara, but her parents stood by her. One day, when Barbara was outside playing a game with the boys, a neighborhood woman called to Barbara to come over. She invited her inside and said, "Barbara, it is time you learned to do the things that girls should be doing!" Barbara stared at the

woman without saying a word. Then she turned around, went home, and told her mother what had happened. Sara McClintock immediately called the neighbor on the telephone. "Don't ever do that again," she told her.

Looking back at her childhood, Barbara said, "I was an oddball. I don't think I was very easy to get along with. But I entertained myself a lot."

The McClintock family spent their summers at the beach, at the far end of Long Beach, on Long Island, New York. These times were sheer joy! Long Beach was natural and untouched country then, a perfect place for the McClintock children to be free. Their beach house was nothing more than a shack, with no running water, and an outhouse. The children had to share beds, sleeping head to foot. Sara often made a game of it, especially when they had friends over, measuring each child to see just how they would fit together on the beds.

They brushed their teeth standing on the jetty and spat the toothpaste into the water. They loved that—and everything about their life at the beach.

Barbara especially loved her times alone. In the mornings she would get up early and walk their dog, Mutty, by the water. In the evenings, when no one could see her, Barbara would go back to the beach by herself. Then she would do a special kind of running that she had made up. She would stand very tall, with her back completely straight, and, looking straight ahead, run in a rhythmic way. It was as if she were floating, or flying. She could run and run without getting tired. She felt a sense of bliss when she was running like that. When she was older, she read a book about Buddhism and found out that in

Tibet, some Buddhist monks called "Running Lamas" run the same way. The Tibetan name for this kind of running is *lung-gom*, which means "meditation on energy." The lamas (or *lung-gom-pa*) were said to have such powers of concentration that they could run very quickly and for very long distances—hundreds of miles at a time. Barbara had discovered an age-old way to meditate, a way to be out of her body and think. This ability to separate from her body would be crucial to her work as a scientist later on.

Although she did enjoy being alone and playing sports with the boys, in many ways it was hard for Barbara to be so different. But she knew she couldn't change. She was lucky that her parents understood that too. Looking back at her childhood, Barbara said, "I would have gone mad if my parents had made me do things I didn't want to do, or not allowed me to do things I wanted to."

CHAPTER 3

Loving to Know Things

As she got older, sports became less important to Barbara. Now she threw herself into learning. It was as if she had decided that if she was going to be different, this was a better way to do it. She still didn't spend time with other girls; and now that she didn't play sports with the boys, she devoted almost all of her time to school.

At Erasmus Hall High School in Brooklyn, she discovered that she loved science and math and was very good at both subjects. Her favorite part was finding problems and solving them. She often solved problems in unusual ways, ways that the teacher hadn't expected. But she begged the teacher to let her do it her way. "It was a tremendous joy," she said, "the whole process of finding that answer, just pure joy."

At home, times were tough again. The United States had entered World War I. Life changed for everyone in America as all efforts went to supporting the war. Food and fuel were rationed, meaning each family was allotted only a certain amount. Most able-bodied men were called to fight or serve in the war. Thomas McClintock was called to duty in Europe as a military surgeon, so the McClintocks lost his doctor's salary. Once again Sara had to give piano lessons to bring in money.

Barbara and her mother fought terribly. Perhaps it was because money was scarce again, and that brought out the worst in Sara; or perhaps it was because Barbara was a teenager, and that brought out the worst in her. But the fights got worse and worse. Marjorie, though she was very close to Sara, would stand up for Barbara when they fought. But it didn't help; Sara still yelled at Barbara. Years later Barbara said that she was able to block out the hurtful things her mother said when they fought. So she didn't remember what her mother had said—she just remembered the terrible fights.

The summer she was fourteen, Barbara had an especially terrible fight with her mother. The family had been invited to a party on the beach. Barbara refused to go. She thought it was silly. "If you won't go like everybody else," yelled Sara, "then you are not a member of this family." She threw Barbara out of the house. Barbara went to an agency that found jobs and rooms for teenage girls. She got a job and lived away from home that summer. But she came back home in Sep-

tember, because she really wanted to go back to high school. Fortunately, Sara let her stay.

Because school was so important to her, Barbara knew she wanted to go to college after high school. But Sara McClintock had other ideas.

Both of Barbara's older sisters, Marjorie and Mignon, had also been very good students in high school. Marjorie was even offered scholarship money to attend a college called Vassar. But like many parents at that time, Sara was worried that if her daughters went to college, they would not be able to find husbands. She persuaded both of them not to go. She told Barbara she could not go to college either.

Barbara, however, was determined to continue her studies. She graduated from high school at age sixteen in the middle of the school year. She got a job, but every night she went to the library. If she couldn't go to college, she was going to teach herself! She kept pushing her mother to let her go to Cornell University, in upstate New York, a good school she had heard was happy to have women as students. Sara steadfastly refused.

Toward the end of that summer, Thomas McClintock came home from the war. He must have taken Barbara's side, for one morning, when Barbara was on her way to work, Sara said, "Dad and I were talking and we decided you should go to college."

As it turned out, Cornell's fall term started the next week—too soon for Barbara to complete all the paperwork needed to enroll. But her parents put her on the train on Monday anyway, and on Tuesday morning she stood in line with all the other *M*'s. When her turn came, the person behind the desk said, "You don't have any papers—how do you expect to get in?"

Just then someone called out, "Barbara McClintock!" The man behind the desk walked away for a minute, came back, and said, "Go ahead." Barbara was in! Barbara never knew exactly what happened in that minute, but she was sure that her mother had done something to get her into Cornell. Although Sara still didn't understand Barbara,

still didn't approve of her choice, she had made sure that Barbara could be just where she wanted to be.

For Barbara, Cornell was like a dream come true. She loved it from her very first class. She was doing exactly what she wanted to be doing—learning new things all the time. She never lost that wonderful feeling all through college.

In fact, she got so absorbed in her work that sometimes she even forget where—or who—she was. When she studied, it was almost as if she were back on the beach doing her running meditation.

One time Barbara had to take a final test for a course in geology (the study of planet Earth), a course that she had really enjoyed. When she got to the classroom, she took the test questions and a blue note-book to write down the answers. She was supposed to write her name on the blue book before she began the test, but she was so eager to take the test that she didn't bother. Barbara wrote and wrote nonstop, enjoying herself tremendously, until she finished the test. When she was done, she turned to the front of the book to write down her name. But she couldn't remember it! She had gotten so absorbed in the test, she had forgotten her own name. She felt as if she had disappeared, that she had become part of the work. She was too embarrassed to ask anybody what her name was, she said later, because "They would think I was cuckoo!" So she just sat there, nervously, hoping that it would come to her. Finally, after twenty minutes, it did.

Barbara actually loved that feeling of losing herself in her work. She resented anything personal that got in her way. That's how she felt about her hair. So, just as she had with her clothes as a child, she de-

cided to break the rules. At that time it was unheard of for a woman to have short hair. Women grew their hair very long, and then spent a lot of time putting it up. But one day Barbara went to the campus barber and had a long talk with him. She convinced him to cut her hair short. What a fuss that made around the campus! Everybody talked about Barbara with the short hair.

Barbara had fun in college outside of classes too. For the first time in her life she made a lot of friends, both women and men. She was so popular that she was elected president of her freshman women's class. Barbara went out on a lot of dates, and even played banjo in a jazz band. She had such a good time that sometimes she forgot to go to classes, and went ice-skating instead.

Then something happened that seems to have changed things. She was going to join a girls' club called a sorority. But when she found out that they wouldn't let her Jewish friends become members, she was very upset. She refused to join. Whether it was that incident, or just the love of knowledge that changed her, by the time she was in her third year of college, Barbara had stopped her social whirligig and was throwing all of her energy into her studies again. She kept playing the banjo at night in a jazz combo, but soon even that would go—for the love of science.

CHAPTER 4

The Mystery of Life

By the time Barbara was in her third year of college, she was fascinated by genetics. Genetics is a branch of biology that studies how parents pass on looks and other features to their children. Geneticists try to answer such questions as, Why do you have a nose like your mother's and curly hair like your father's? Why is your sister tall, like your grandfather, but you're short? How can two brown-eyed parents have a child with blue eyes? How can two black dogs have a brown puppy? Barbara felt that genetics would someday unravel the mystery of life.

In 1923 Barbara decided to enroll in graduate school to study genetics. But there was a problem. At Cornell, genetics was taught in the plant-breeding department. That's because scientists did their experiments on plants, mostly on maize, the kind of corn with many-colored kernels. (Maize is sometimes called Indian corn—people use it to decorate their houses around Halloween and Thanksgiving.) But the plant-breeding department didn't take women as students. Probably they felt that working in cornfields just wasn't "ladylike." Today, there are laws against that kind of discrimination. Back then there were no such laws. The people in the plant-breeding department could tell Barbara, a top student, that she couldn't enroll in their graduate school just because she was a woman.

Barbara had never let the fact that she was female stop her before. She found a way to work around the rules. Barbara had also enjoyed cytology, the study of cells. All living things are made of cells. Fortunately for Barbara, cytology was taught in the botany department. Women were allowed in the botany department, so Barbara enrolled in it to study cytology. She took courses in the plant-breeding department, too, so she could study genetics. Combining genetics and cytology turned out to be a winning move.

Genetics was a very new science. It had been discovered only sixty years before by Gregor Mendel. Mendel (1822–1884) was a monk who worked in the garden of his monastery in Austria. He noticed some interesting things about the peas he was growing. Some pea plants were tall. Some were short. Some pea pods were plump, some were pinched. Some peas were smooth, others were wrinkled. There were green peas and yellow peas. There were purple pea flowers and white pea flowers.

Mendel was curious. What made all these differences? He decided to try some experiments. He bred pea plants, using, for exam-

ple, a tall pea plant and a short pea plant as parents for a new plant. You might think that a tall plant and a short plant would make a medium plant. But all the new plants were tall. Mendel wondered why. So he bred those tall plants with each other. More tall plants? Well, most of them were tall, but some of them were short. Mendel spent years breeding and crossbreeding pea plants. With a lot of work (and math), he figured out some of the rules that dictate how parent pea plants pass on traits (such as height or color) to their offspring.

In 1865 Mendel wrote a paper to tell scientists about his discoveries. No one understood what he was talking about, so they ignored him. Mendel went back to being a monk.

In 1900, two years before Barbara McClintock was born, scientists finally realized that Mendel had been right. They gave the name "gene" to the unit that carries a trait. A plant has a "tall" gene or a "short" gene; a "plump" gene or a "pinched" gene; a "smooth" gene or a "wrinkled" gene. A person has a gene for curly hair or for straight hair, a gene for tallness or for shortness, etc. By the time Barbara became a graduate student, scientists were trying to learn exactly where genes were inside living things and exactly how genes worked. Just as when her uncle had tried to figure out how the motor of his new truck worked, Barbara was right there under the hood.

But instead of looking under a hood at a mechanical motor, she was looking through a microscope at living things, at cells. Scientists could see that in every cell there was a nucleus. They could also see that in every nucleus were some stringy things. To see the workings of the cell better, scientists had developed a way to dye the cells. The stringy things absorbed the dye so well that scientists named them "chromosomes," from the Greek words for "color" and "body."

By looking at cells under a microscope, scientists could see that chromosomes are important when cells divide and make new cells. They thought chromosomes might have something to do with passing traits from parent to child. But they didn't know what chromosomes did or how they did it.

In her first year as a graduate student, Barbara McClintock brought them one step closer.

To earn some money, Barbara got a job working for a cytologist (a scientist who studies cells) after classes. He was looking at cells of the maize plant under a microscope. He and other maize cytologists were trying to solve a mystery. They knew each maize cell had ten chromosomes. But they couldn't tell them apart. They wanted to be able to label them and number them. That way they might be able to

figure out what each chromosome did. But so far they hadn't been able to. In fact, it seemed impossible.

Working after classes, Barbara watched what her boss was doing. She stained cells the way he taught her to, but she could tell that his technique was not good enough. "He was looking at the wrong place," she said. So, on her own, she tried something new. Using her new staining technique, Barbara found the right place to look. She could see clearly the different sizes, lengths, and shapes of the chromosomes. Just as when she was in high school, Barbara had not gone about solving the problem in the usual way. She had chosen her own way to solve it. And because she had, at age twenty-one she had done what none of the older, more experienced scientists had been able to do. She had identified and numbered the ten chromosomes of maize!

Believe it or not, the cytologist she worked for was furious that she had beaten him to it. It was the end of her job with him, but the beginning of her career. Other maize cytologists were thrilled. Now they could work out what each of the ten chromosomes did and what role they played in genetics.

CHAPTER 5

It's A-Maizing!

Barbara was not only very good at looking at cells under the microscope and at solving difficult technical problems in the laboratory. She was also willing and able to do the hard physical work in the cornfield. Maize geneticists performed their experiments by planting maize plants and then crossbreeding them, just as Mendel had done with his peas. Maize is very good for studying genetics because of the many-colored kernels. Each ear of corn has a different pattern of colors. In one ear of corn, for example, some kernels may be purple, some may be darker purple, some may be red, and some may have yellow splotches. The kernels also have different textures. How do they get those patterns and textures? Just like people and pea plants, maize plants get their traits from their parents. Barbara and other maize geneticists wanted to figure out exactly how that happened.

Barbara took an ear of corn. She looked at the kernels. She saw one that had mostly purple kernels. Then she took a flower from the tassel of that corn plant and put a section of it under a microscope. She looked at the chromosomes. She made notes to remember exactly what each of the chromosomes looked like. How long was it? Was it straight? Did it have any knobs on it? Where were the knobs?

Then she looked at the chromosomes from a plant whose kernels were purple, red, and yellow. She marked down what those chromosomes looked like.

Next she asked herself, What if I crossed those two plants? What would the kernels of the offspring look like? What would the chromosomes look like? She took a kernel from each of those ears of corn. She carefully planted them, marking exactly which plant each was from. (She often worked on hundreds of corn plants at a time.)

In a few weeks the corn plants had grown and it was time for them to breed. Barbara had to work quickly and carefully in the cornfield. A corn plant has both female and male parts. The female part of the plant is in the ear, or cob, of the corn. The male part is the pollen in the tassel—the bundle of stringy fibers at the top of the plant. When a corn plant grows, the cob grows too. But it is very tiny before it is fertilized. In order to be fertilized, it puts out silks. (If you've ever husked an ear of corn, you've seen the silks. They're the thin, hairlike, silky strands right next to the kernels.)

In nature, a corn plant fertilizes itself or the plants next to it. When the wind blows, pollen from the tassels blows onto the silks of nearby ears of corn. To control which pollen fertilized which ear of corn, Barbara put a small paper bag over each ear before the silks came out. As the ear grew and the silk developed, no pollen touched it. She also put a bigger brown-paper bag (like a lunch bag) over the top of each tassel. She fastened it shut with a staple or paper clip, so all of the yellow pollen would come off into the bag.

When she was ready to pollinate the plants, she took the bag off the tassel of one plant. Then she pulled the bag off the ear of corn of the other plant. She poured the yellow pollen onto the ear. That pollen would then fertilize that ear of corn. Quickly she put the bigger bag over the ear of corn, so no other pollen from another plant could contaminate it. When that ear of corn grew, it was the offspring, or child, of the two plants whose chromosomes Barbara had looked at the year before.

As Barbara found out, this was very hard work. She had to do all of the pollinating in a few weeks. She worked twelve-hour days in the cornfields, driving the hundred miles there and back every three days in her Model A Ford. In the fall she would harvest the corn. Then she would spend the winter looking at the corn under a microscope to see what the chromosomes looked like.

Barbara worked very hard during her graduate-school years, and the harder she worked the happier she was. She made friends with the other maize geneticists, friends she would keep for a lifetime.

She went to her parents' house or to her sister Marjorie's house for vacations, but her home was really at Cornell. Visits with her mother were strained, because Sara still thought her daughter should be getting married and having babies, not tromping around in cornfields and looking through microscopes. Thomas was encouraging, though. Right before she was to take her final exams to get her advanced degree, he sent her a poem that started:

> The best good fortune we can hope
> Is when you meet them, you can cope
> With every one, or all the bunch;
> Believe me, I have got the hunch
> There's not a single Prof. who roams
> Who knows as well his Chromosomes . . .

Barbara did know her chromosomes. She got her graduate degree in 1927 and stayed on at Cornell to continue her work with maize. Barbara was as happy as she could be. She was getting paid to do what she loved best: think about things and solve problems. As usual, Barbara worked hard—and played hard, too. She was an excellent and energetic tennis player. Everyday when they were done working, Barbara and her new friend, a graduate student named Harriet Creighton, played tennis. Although Harriet was much taller than Bar-

bara, Barbara played with such energy that Harriet was exhausted after their matches.

Barbara and Harriet were a good team in the lab, too. It wasn't long before they made a very big discovery. Geneticists thought that when cells divide to produce new cells, some of their chromosomes exchange genetic information. This is what they thought—but nobody had been able to show that it definitely happened. With Harriet's help, Barbara set out to prove it. She and other scientists believed that chromosomes exchanged information when they crossed over each other. They thought it occurred this way: one gene, say a gene for a red kernel, is on one part of one chromosome. The gene for a waxy-feeling kernel is on a part of another chromosome. If the two chromosomes crossed over each other at the right places when the cells divided, then the offspring would have kernels that were red and waxy. Many scientists all over the world were trying to prove this.

Barbara and Harriet did it first! Barbara saw a knob on the short arm of chromosome number nine, and an extension on its long arm. By watching to see if offspring had that knob, Barbara could tell how chromosomes pass on genetic information. In 1931 Barbara and Harriet published a paper proving that chromosomes *do* cross over and exchange information. Now it was certain that genes were on chromosomes and that the genes determine which traits are passed on to offspring.

The following year Barbara and Harriet presented their discovery to a meeting of scientists. It made a big splash! In fact, their discovery became the basis of modern genetics.

Now all geneticists knew what her friends at Cornell already knew: that Barbara McClintock was a brilliant, hardworking scientist who had a great future ahead of her.

Barbara's parents soon found out too. A scientist who had heard Barbara and Harriet present their paper took a ship back to Europe afterward. As luck would have it, on that same ship were Sara and Thomas McClintock, on vacation. When the scientist found out that Barbara McClintock's parents were on the ship, he made sure to meet them. He excitedly congratulated them on their daughter's great scientific success. That chance meeting wiped away all their worries about the choices their oddball daughter had made.

CHAPTER 6

No Job For a Woman

You would think that after such a great success, universities and research centers all over the country would have wanted to hire Barbara. But that didn't happen—because she was a woman. Most scientists at that time didn't think that a woman would be a serious scientist for long. They expected even brilliant young women to marry, have babies, and give up science. So they didn't want to hire them. But Barbara was not interested in getting married. Her work was the most important thing to her.

If she had liked teaching, she could have gotten a job as a professor at a women's college. Lots of women scientists, including Harriet Creighton, did that. But Barbara didn't want to teach. She was not comfortable in the classroom. Her place was in the cornfield and the laboratory. She wanted to plant her corn and study it.

Since she couldn't get a permanent full-time job, she divided her time and research between Cornell, the University of Missouri, and the California Institute of Technology, driving around the country in her sporty Model A Roadster. She wished she had a home base, but as

long as she could plant her corn and look through her microscope, she was happy. Fortunately her family was able to give her money, because without a regular job, she did not get regular pay.

For a while it looked as though she would get a permanent job at the University of Missouri. The administrators there didn't mind that she was a woman. But Barbara was too "weird" and "unladylike" for them. One day she forgot to bring the keys to her lab. Rather than take away from precious work time to go back home for her keys, she climbed in through the window. Why not? Well, not everybody thought that was a sensible thing to do. Someone passing by saw her and told everyone about it. They were shocked. No professor—and certainly no woman—should do such a thing. Even though Barbara was becoming more and more well-known in her field (in 1939 she was elected vice-president of the Genetics Society of America), there

Barbara
McClintock
worked
here.

COLD SPRING HARBOR

was no future for her at the University of Missouri. Soon afterward another, less successful woman was given the job that Barbara was expecting to get. In 1941 Barbara left for good. She didn't know where she was going, but she knew she had to leave.

She spent that summer working at Cold Spring Harbor Laboratory on Long Island. Cold Spring Harbor is a scientific community nestled by the water about forty miles east of New York City. During the summer it bustles with scientists and students from all over the world, who come to work and study. During the winter it is a quiet and peaceful place for the few scientists who stay. For many scientists it is heaven. For Barbara it certainly was. She liked it so much that she stayed after that summer—and never left. Fortunately for Barbara, the director of the genetics department at Cold Spring Harbor recognized her genius. So, too, did the Carnegie Institution of Washington, D.C., which then funded Cold Spring Harbor. The Carnegie Institution was thrilled to have Barbara at Cold Spring Harbor and gave her money for her research for the rest of her working life.

The other geneticists at Cold Spring Harbor knew they had gotten a great thing in Barbara McClintock. One man, when he heard that Barbara was staying, jumped into the air and shouted, "We should mark today's date with red letters in the Department calendar!"

But Barbara was lonely at first at Cold Spring Harbor, partly because she was the only maize geneticist there. She missed her friends at Cornell; she missed having people to talk to about her work. She missed playing tennis with her friend Harriet Creighton. Still, she was happy with her work. She had space to grow her corn, equipment to study it with, and money to live on. The Carnegie Institution funded her and left her alone. That was just what she needed.

CHAPTER 7

Jumping Genes

Unlike most scientists, Barbara liked to work alone, with little help from assistants or students. Many people thought her style of working was strange, but she wanted to do every bit of the work herself. She did tasks that most scientists gave to students to do, such as planting the seeds and getting the slides ready for the microscope. Barbara felt that by doing everything, she really got to know her plants. And the better she knew them, the more she noticed. She wanted to be aware of even the smallest details, because she knew they provided the clues to the larger whole. She noticed the slightest variations in kernel or leaf color. Through the microscope, she looked for the small changes in chromosomes that might mean big changes in the corn.

Because of her attention to detail, and her brilliance, her reputation grew and grew. People knew Barbara could see things that no one else could.

In 1944 one of her old Cornell friends, George Beadle, asked her to come out to Stanford University in California for a few weeks to help him with a problem. Beadle, who later won a Nobel Prize for his work, was studying *Neurospora*, a red mold that grows on bread. (So those things growing in your refrigerator really are science experiments in the making!) He was trying to identify and label all of the chromosomes in *Neurospora*, just as Barbara had done for maize. He

wanted to solve the mystery of how *Neurospora* worked. But the *Neurospora* chromosomes were so small that even with the strongest microscope available, no scientist had been able to do it. Beadle knew that if anybody could solve this problem, Barbara McClintock could.

When she got to California, Barbara worked very hard, looking at *Neurospora* cells on slides, but she just couldn't see the chromosomes clearly. One day, feeling very discouraged, she left the lab and went for a walk down a long road lined with giant eucalyptus trees. She sat on a bench under the eucalyptus trees for half an hour, thinking, but not really knowing what she was thinking. She even cried a little bit. At the end of that half hour she got up and went back to the lab.

Under the microscope, the chromosomes seemed to get bigger and bigger. She felt as if she were right down there with them. Just like the time in college when she had gotten so excited about the questions on the test that she forgot her name, she lost herself in her work; she actually became part of it. Although it was her years of experience that enabled her to solve the mystery, Barbara always felt that she couldn't have done it without that half hour under the eucalyptus trees.

Now she was able to see the chromosomes on the slides as she couldn't before. She could tell them apart, and see what happened to each one as the cells divided. Within five days she was able to show her friend George Beadle not only the seven chromosomes of *Neurospora*, but also how *Neurospora* made new cells.

This success gave Barbara real confidence in her ability as a scientist. It was with great excitement that she returned to Cold Spring Harbor and her maize. She was ready to settle down and really work!

Back in her cornfields, Barbara knew every single plant in her field from seed to cob, kernel by kernel, chromosome by chromosome. And she remembered everything about their parents and grandparents and great-grandparents, too. Because she knew her plants so well, she started noticing things that nobody else would have noticed. On some plants she saw strange patterns in the colors of the kernels. On the same plants she saw strange blotches of color on the leaves and corn stalks.

Barbara knew something was going on, and she suspected it was something very unusual. When she began to look at the chromosomes of those plants, she was sure of it. Something was happening that scientists were certain was impossible. That is often how great discoveries in science are made. Everybody thinks a certain thing is true, that it is a firm rule. Then one scientist is able to see what nobody else can see—the rule being broken.

At that time scientists thought genes were lined up on chromosomes like beads on a string. They thought each gene had its place and that it never moved. But from what Barbara could tell by looking at corn kernels and chromosomes, genes did move. Sometimes they jumped around on the chromosome. Sometimes they even jumped from one chromosome to another. When the genes jumped, weird things happened.

Barbara became more and more convinced that genes were not like beads on a string. The way she saw them was more like children in a line. The teacher says, "Class, stay in line as we walk to the auditorium." But as the class is walking, Billy jumps out of his place in line and runs up to Kate. He tells her to kick John. Kate jumps out of her place, goes behind John, and kicks him. John starts crying and punches Emily. Then Emily runs to the nurse's office and the whole class runs with her.

Barbara saw changes in corn kernels and chromosomes that made her think there were two kinds of genes that jumped. One jumped first, like Billy, and made a second one, like Kate, jump. When a gene jumped into or near another gene, that gene acted odd, either by jumping itself, like Kate, or doing something weird and unexpected, like John's punching Emily. Then the whole line acted strange like running to the nurse's office instead of the auditorium.

Barbara called these jumping genes "transposable elements," or "transposons." She was very excited by her discovery. She knew it was very important. What it showed her was that these moving genes could cause offspring to have entirely new traits—traits that could not be explained by Mendel's rules. If jumping genes caused strange patterns on corn, then they could also cause other unexpected genetic traits that scientists had not been able to explain, such as a different eye color in a fruit fly, or weird wing shape.

There are always surprising characteristics in offspring, surprising because they had not been predicted by the scientists studying the plant or animal. Barbara now knew that jumping genes caused at least some of these surprises. By jumping from one place on the chromosome to another, the transposons regulated why some traits showed

up one way one time and another way another time. What Barbara saw was a system of control and regulation among genes.

To be absolutely certain there was no better explanation for the patterns on her corn, Barbara planted more maize and studied more chromosomes. She knew that she had to do many experiments and careful observations. In 1950, when she was ready, she wrote a short paper about her transposable elements and sent it to a scientific journal. Though it was published, few scientists read it and even fewer understood its importance. She decided that she needed to be able to tell her ideas to a wide audience.

In the summer of 1951 she got her chance. There was going to be a big meeting of scientists at Cold Spring Harbor. Geneticists were coming from all over the world. It would be the perfect time to tell about her discovery. At scientific meetings, a scientist gets up in front of the group and reads a paper out loud, like an oral report in school. After the scientist is finished, others ask questions and discuss the paper. It is that exciting exchange of ideas that helps a paper make a big splash, ensuring that it will make a difference in the way other scientists think and work all over the world. Barbara was very nervous before her speech. She knew that if she could get her point across, it would make her career—and, more importantly, change the way people thought about genes. But if she bombed, her career could be ruined.

It was a warm summer day. Barbara McClintock stepped to the front of the auditorium. At forty-nine, she was already a well-known and respected scientist. But she knew that what she was about to tell her audience was the biggest discovery of her life. She looked out at the crowded room. Most of the top scientists in genetics were there. Many of the faces were familiar. Some were famous. Some were friends. Barbara looked down at her paper nervously. She cleared her throat to begin.

At first her fellow scientists listened eagerly, their eyes bright, their heads nodding. But before long their eyes began to glaze over.

Some of them yawned. One or two might even have fallen asleep. At the end of her speech it was time for questions. Not a single person raised his hand. That was a bad sign.

Barbara looked out at her audience. Some of the scientists were staring at her in anger. Others seemed to be laughing. She heard someone say, "What is she talking about?"

Her speech had bombed.

Why? There were several reasons. One was Barbara's fault. She understood what she was saying, but she told it in such a complicated way that almost nobody in the audience could follow her. Since she was so used to working alone, she didn't have much practice explaining her work to others, especially not to a large audience.

Another reason her speech failed was the fault of the other scientists. Their minds were closed. What Barbara said went against everything they believed. They *knew* that genes could not jump around. They thought Barbara McClintock had gone mad! Because her conclusion seemed impossible, they didn't try to understand her evidence. That is why they didn't ask her any questions.

Barbara McClintock knew that to be a good scientist you have to keep your mind open to all kinds of possibilities. She once told a friend who was trying to solve a problem, "Look at the facts you have. Use your imagination to link them as well as you can. Then use your imagination to leap from the facts you have to the next fact you do not have yet. See where it is and then go find it." The scientists in her audience didn't do that. But Barbara had, and she knew she was right.

Barbara was more surprised than upset that she hadn't been able to convince the other scientists. Unlike Mendel, she did not give up. She worked on her theory some more and presented it again five years later. The scientific world ignored her again.

This time they just weren't paying attention. Biologists and geneticists were all very excited about something else, something called DNA. The chemical that chromosomes are made of, DNA is like the instruction booklet for how traits are passed on. In 1953, three years before Barbara's second attempt to explain transposable elements, James Watson and Francis Crick figured out the structure of DNA. Once they knew what DNA looked like, scientists could determine how it passed on genetic information. This was very exciting. To most people it was far more exciting than old-fashioned maize genetics. Everyone was calling DNA the secret of life.

Barbara McClintock was interested in DNA too, but she knew she could help unravel the secret of life right there in her maize. Besides, her evidence for jumping genes was so strong, she just had to keep working on it. "When you feel that strongly about something," she said, "you can't be turned off. Nobody can hurt you. You just go right on; you don't even feel it."

CHAPTER 8

She Was Right!

Barbara stopped trying to convince anyone about jumping genes. Fortunately, the Carnegie Institution kept paying her. So day after day, year after year, Barbara McClintock planted her corn and studied it, even though the scientific world ignored her. "It was fun," she said. "I couldn't wait to get up in the morning."

When she wasn't working, she spent time with friends, played her banjo, took long walks in the woods, did exercises, and read a lot. She read about Tibetan Buddhism; she read about Indian culture; she read about real-life murders; and she read a lot of scientific papers.

In 1960 she read a scientific paper that excited her tremendously. Two French scientists had described a system of controlling and regulating genes in bacteria. Although they did not describe jumping genes, they did describe a system in which some genes controlled other genes. Unlike Barbara, who still used the same old microscopes she always had, these scientists (and most others) were using much more powerful microscopes. With these electron microscopes, scientists could see the tiniest bits of matter in cells. Although they couldn't actually see the "controlling elements," as they called them, they saw what they felt was indisputable evidence of their existence.

Barbara wrote an article explaining that what they had seen was similar to her discovery. The two French scientists, Jacques Monod and François Jacob, read her papers. The following summer, in 1961, at another meeting at Cold Spring Harbor, Monod and Jacob gave Barbara McClintock credit for having discovered transposable elements ten years earlier. Barbara also gave a speech explaining how her work fit with theirs. The other scientists at the meeting were excited— but not about Barbara's work; they were excited about Jacob and Monod's discovery. Only a very few scientists saw the importance of what Barbara was saying.

That was her last attempt to convince others of her discovery. Barbara kept on doing her experiments, and filing her results in a drawer. Once a year she published her findings in the yearbook of the Carnegie Institution. But the yearbook was not something scientists read.

In the 1970s, some two decades after her first speech at Cold Spring Harbor, Barbara McClintock's work started to be recognized by more scientists. At first they thought that jumping genes were very rare, that they didn't occur often, and therefore were not important. But as biology got more advanced, other scientists started seeing transposons in bacteria and yeast and fruit flies. Slowly, slowly, more scientists started to understand the importance of jumping genes.

Finally, by the end of the 1970s and the beginning of the 1980s, scientists realized how important jumping genes were. They could see that jumping genes explained many different kinds of genetic mutations, or changes. No more would scientists think of genes as unmoving beads on a string. They moved, just as Barbara McClintock had said way back in 1951, and that movement made all the difference. It would take many more studies, but scientists now knew that jumping genes play a very important role in evolution, in how bacteria become resistant to antibiotics, and how normal cells become cancerous.

Barbara was very pleased that the world had finally caught up with her. But she didn't want to be famous. Not at all. She didn't want anything to get in the way of her work. For even though she was in her seventies, Barbara worked every day, and she worked hard.

But with acceptance came fame, and in 1981, when she was seventy-nine, she won eight awards, several of which came with a lot of money.

She bought herself a new car and moved to a bigger apartment closer to her laboratory. Other than that she didn't change a thing about her life. But her life changed anyway. All of a sudden she was getting phone calls from reporters who wanted to write articles about her, letters from people asking her questions, letters from people who knew her when she was a child, and at Cornell, and at other times in her life. She even got letters asking for money. All of this attention ruined what she prized most—being left alone to work.

She hated being famous.

And it was about to get worse.

On October 10, 1983, Barbara McClintock was going through her usual morning routine with the radio on. If she had had a telephone at home, she would have gotten a personal call. But Barbara did not like to be disturbed by telephone calls. So instead, she heard on the radio: "Barbara McClintock has won the Nobel Prize in the category of Physiology or Medicine."

Most people, when they hear they have won the Nobel Prize, the highest prize in the world, shout and cheer and celebrate. Barbara McClintock said, "Oh dear." Then, after doing her aerobics, she got dressed—in her usual baggy blue jeans, shirt, and work shoes—and went for a walk picking walnuts. She thought she might bake walnut cake for her friends, as she often did. Later that day she would talk to reporters. But for now she wanted time alone to think.

Each year the Nobel Prize is given to the people in the world the Nobel Committee feel have benefited humankind the most. Getting the prize says, basically, "You have done it. You are the best in your field." Winners get a lot of money, and a lot of attention. People all over the world want to meet them, talk to them, take their pictures.

Barbara was proud to win the award. She was the first woman to win an unshared Nobel Prize in the category of Physiology or Medicine. She was only the third woman to win an unshared Nobel Prize in any science category. People usually win the award a few years after they have made a big discovery. It is very unusual to win the award for a discovery made three decades earlier. It was truly a great honor.

When she met with reporters later in the day, she told them, "Yes, I'll go to Stockholm to accept the award. Of course."

The Nobel Prize ceremonies in Stockholm are very fancy. The award winners march into the Stockholm Concert Hall while an orchestra plays grand music. The King of Sweden himself presents the award certificate and gold medal. Afterward the Nobel Laureates feast at a great banquet in their honor. The next day the winners receive their prize money. It was $190,000 the year Barbara McClintock won.

Barbara seemed to have a good time at the festivities on December 10, 1983. And though the other winners (all men) were certainly deserving, she was clearly the star of the show. The audience of 1,800 people clapped loudest and longest for the eighty-one-year-old woman who had discovered jumping genes—more than thirty years earlier.

AFTERWORD

After winning the Nobel Prize, Barbara McClintock became something of a legend. Her picture appeared in newspapers all over the world—a little old lady holding an ear of maize. Scientists made sure to visit her when they came to Cold Spring Harbor. When they did, Barbara McClintock gave them her time, her knowledge, and her help. One scientist who came to work at Cold Spring Harbor in the last years of Barbara's life said, "She was the most brilliant person I ever met. And she was incredibly kind and helpful to me and all young scientists. She was not only good at her own work, she was good at other people's work too."

Friends described her as forceful and strong-willed, but also as gentle, loving, and sweet. One friend said, "She taught me how to stand up for myself." Another friend said, "If she passed you outside, she would always point out something—a flower, a leaf—and explain it to you." She had a special feeling for plants—and sometimes she felt that plants themselves had feelings. She once said that she hated to walk on grass because she could almost hear it screaming!

Barbara McClintock not only had great vision in her work; she noticed everything in everyday life, too. She noticed new flowers budding on the Cold Spring Harbor campus, who was wearing earrings and who wasn't, and who needed a kind word, a friend. She remembered every detail about people she had met fifteen years before.

She also had a great sense of humor. The day after she heard she had won the Nobel Prize, she was invited to a party. Not wanting to be recognized, she went wearing a Groucho Marx mask!

Barbara McClintock did her aerobics, visited her friends, and worked on her maize almost until the day she died. She died on September 2, 1992, after being sick for only one day. She was ninety years old.

When she died, newspapers and magazines all over the world wrote about "the corn lady." Scientists called her "one of the most important figures in the history of genetics," and "the most important figure in biology in general." At Cold Spring Harbor they held a memorial service. There was lively banjo music. Friends told stories and talked about the brilliant woman who was "small in size, but great in stature."

Barbara McClintock's work lives on. Before she died, she gave away kernels of her corn. All over the world there are scientists planting and studying the descendants of Barbara's maize. They read her scientific papers, understanding them more now than when she first wrote them. Many people feel that Barbara McClintock was way ahead of her time. Scientists are still learning from her discovery of transposable elements. Special scientific meetings are held just to discuss jumping genes. In years to come, as scientists study evolution, genetic diseases, and cancer, Barbara McClintock's jumping genes will be at the center of their research. They may well be a clue to curing cancer, AIDS, and other diseases.

Barbara McClintock was once asked whether she would live her life any differently if she had it do it over. "I've had such a good time," she said, "I can't imagine having a better life."

INDEX/GLOSSARY

FURTHER READING

To find out more about Barbara McClintock, the science of genetics, and other women scientists, look for more books at your library or bookstore. Here are a few to get you started. You might also want to check out books on other subjects mentioned in this biography, such as botany, or other scientists, such as Gregor Mendel.

Barbara McClintock by Mary Kittredge
(New York: Chelsea House, 1991). Another look at the life and work of Barbara McClintock, with a useful chronology at the end.

The Cartoon Guide to Genetics by Larry Gonick and Mark Wheelis
(New York: HarperCollins, 1991). Although written for adults, this is a very clear and funny introduction to the history of genetics.

A Feeling for the Organism: The Life and Work of Barbara McClintock by Evelyn Fox Keller
(New York: W. H. Freeman and Company Publishers). A wonderful adult biography of Barbara McClintock. Suggest it to a grown-up who would like to know more about her.

Heredity by Dennis Fradin
(New York: Children's Press, 1992). This is a good, basic look at heredity. The big type might make you think the book is too young for you, but it explains a lot of complicated ideas very well.

They Came From DNA by Billy Aronson
(New York: W. H. Freeman and Company Publishers, 1993). A funny and very informative book that takes you down many paths in genetics. Told by a space alien!

The Triumph of Discovery: Women Scientists Who Won the Nobel Prize by Joan Dash
(New York: Julian Messner, 1991). Profiles Barbara McClintock and other women who have won the Nobel Prize.

Winners: Women and the Nobel Prize by Barbara Shiels
(New York: Dillon Press, 1985). A collection about women who have won the Nobel Prize.